From Seed to Crop

Teaching Tips

Blue Level 4

This book focuses on the phonemes **/ow/oi/**.

Before Reading

- Discuss the title. Ask readers what they think the book will be about. Have them briefly explain why.
- Ask readers to point to and say the names of the objects on page 3. On a separate sheet of paper, have them write the words.

Read the Book

- Encourage readers to break down unfamiliar words into units of sound. Then, ask them to string the sounds together to create the words.
- Urge readers to point out when the focused phonics phonemes appear in the text.

After Reading

- Encourage children to reread the book independently or with a friend.
- Ask readers to name other words with /ow/ or /oi/ phonemes. On a separate sheet of paper, have them write the words.

This edition is published by arrangement with Booklife Publishing.

5357 Penn Avenue South
Minneapolis, MN 55419
www.jumplibrary.com

Decodables by Jump! are published by Jump! Library.

Library of Congress Cataloging-in-Publication Data is available at www.loc.gov or upon request from the publisher.

ISBN: 979-8-88524-739-9 (hardcover)
ISBN: 979-8-88524-740-5 (paperback)
ISBN: 979-8-88524-741-2 (ebook)

Photo Credits

Images are courtesy of Shutterstock.com. With thanks to Getty Images, Thinkstock Photo and iStockphoto. Cover - Ian 2010, Vasenina Daria, melaics, irin-k, VIEW17. 3 – Phant, Italian Food Production, Henning Marquardt, domnitsky, Elena Zajchikova, Spiroview Inc. 4&5 - Yellow Cat, Imfoto, somkanae sawatdinak, Sergiy Kuzmin. 6&7 – amenic181, Ramil gibadullin. 8&9 – kram-9, Oleg Mikhaylov. 10&11 – fotohunter. 12&13 – Dzha33, Tatiana Bobkova. 14&15 – stevemart, fizkes.

How many words can you list with **oi** in them?

This is a seed. We can get a crop from the seed.

How will the crop look when it is big?

The seed can go down in the soil.

Seeds can go in a pot too. Soil must be in the pot.

Soon, the crop will join the top of the soil. It will go up and up.

The crop needs liquid to get big.
The soil must be moist.

The crop needs light from the Sun to get big.

The crop gets food from the Sun.

We can pick it off the crop when it is red.

Now it is red. We can pick it off!

It went from green to red. Now it is big. Wow!

Now we have a lot of food. What can we do with it?

Can you sort the words on this page into two groups?

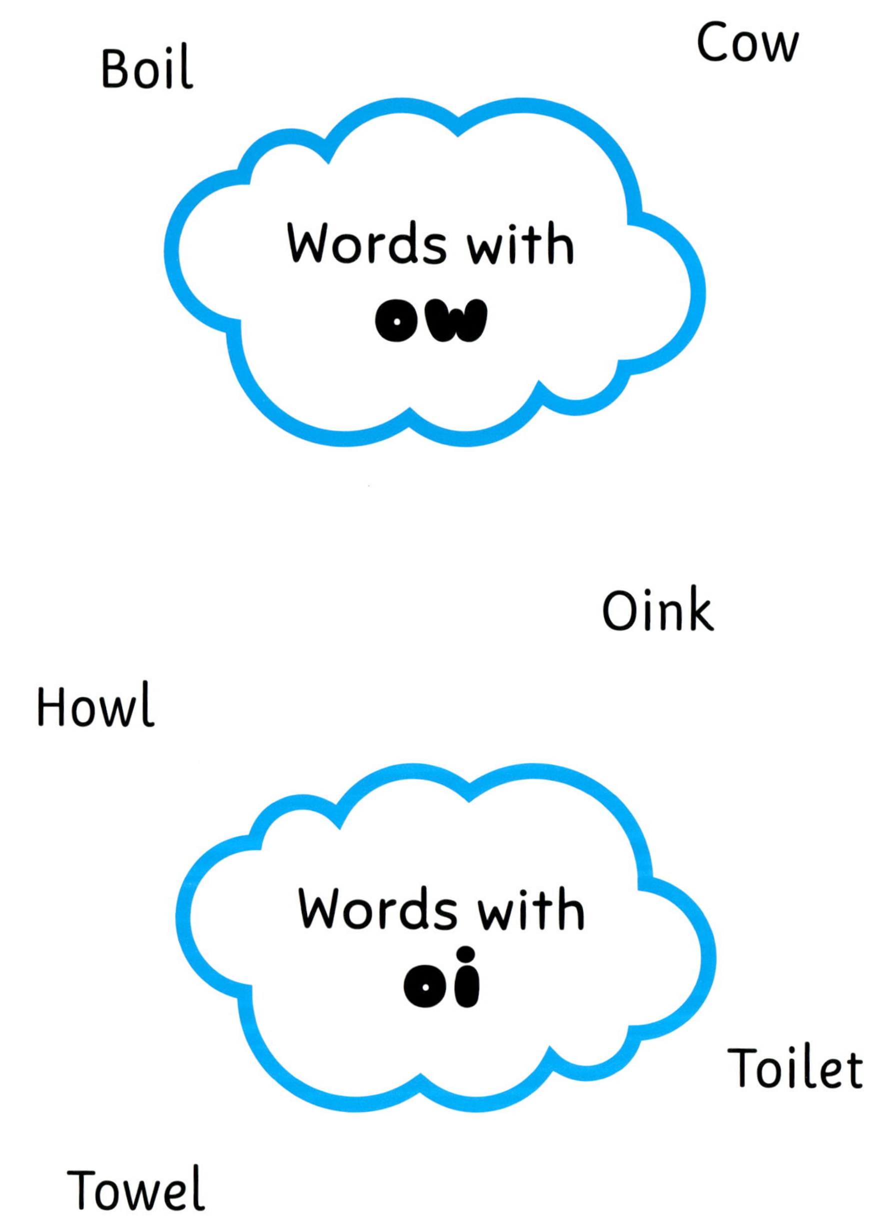